The Life of an Entrepreneur

The hardships of the life,
The loneliness that he feels sometimes

Markus Edison

MP Publishing

Copyright

© 2018 by Markus Edison

TABLE OF CONTENTS

INTRODUCTION 5

WHAT DOES IT MEAN TO BE ENTREPRENEURIAL? 9

BUSINESS STRATEGY 11

I.   THE THREE MAJOR REASONS FOR NEW BUSINESS FAILURE.........12

A.   LACK OF PLANNING 12

B.   INSUFFICIENT FUNDING (UNDERCAPITALIZATION).....................13

C.   OVER REACHING 15

II. THINGS YOU MUST DO TO IMPROVE YOUR BUSINESS: 16

III. "THINK BIG" 17

A.   THE INABILITY TO OUTGROW ENVIRONMENT 18

B.   LACK OF MOTIVATION TO PURSUE BIG IDEAS.........................19

C.   LACK THE SELF-CONFIDENCE 20

D.   LACK THE DIVERSITY AND EXPERTISE...............................21

IV. MINDSET OF SUCCESSFUL ENTREPRENEUR 22

A.   CRITICISM 23

B.   FAILURE 25

C.   OFFENDING OTHERS 27

D.   THE PAST AND THE FUTURE 28

E.   NEGATIVITY 29

V. THE HARSH REALITY OF ENTREPRENEURIAL WORLD 30

A. EXPECT THAT THE FIRST ITERATION OF AN IDEA IS WRONG 31

B. YOUR FAMILY OR FRIENDS CAN'T UNDERSTAND YOU NO MATTER WHAT YOU DO 31

C. YOU WILL MAKE A SMALL WAGE FOR A WHILE............................32

D. YOU CAN'T DO IT ALL YOURSELF 33

E. THERE'S NO SUCH THING AS AN OVERNIGHT SUCCESS 34

F. THERE ARE THINGS THAT ARE NOT COVERED BY YOUR CONTROL 35

VI. HOW TO AVOID THE LONELY LIFE OF AN ENTREPRENEUR...........36

A. CHOOSE A GOOD COMMUNITY 37

B. COLLABORATE 38

C. RELATIONSHIP IS ALWAYS YOUR PRIORITY 39

D. CO-WORKING SPACES 40

E. BE MORE ASSERTIVE AND HAVING FORCEFUL PERSONALITY..........40

F. LEARN FROM YOUR MENTOR..41

G. BE TRUE TO YOURSELF..41

ABOUT THE AUTHOR 43

INTRODUCTION

Being entrepreneur to think differently from the others is the unique ability that you can use to improve your career. While other people are satisfied with what the status of their lives, the entrepreneur will take risk to grow their career. They are not looking for a job; they are the ones who create the job. They do not work for their boss; they are the boss of their own business. They do not pay based on the month or day they went to work; their income is directly related to the efforts and perseverance they dedicated for the success of their business. They are free to do everything they want to do, wherever they want and in how they will begin. Most entrepreneurs do not consider their actual work as just a source of financial necessity because most of the entrepreneurs do these things because this is something they love.

How does entrepreneur mind develop? The viewpoint and discussions in this question are very broad and never ends. Some people believe that entrepreneurs have the characteristics of being entrepreneurs from the moment they were born and continue to improve as they grow together with the right mix of experience and effort. As well as others believe that being an entrepreneur you need to go through a variety of training, research and continuous learning about business.

But actually the idea that entrepreneurs were born with the characteristics of being entrepreneur at the beginning was extremely ridiculous. Contrary to some opinions and false beliefs, entrepreneurship can be taught and can be learned based on how much you want it to know. In fact one of the key drivers of our economy is entrepreneurship. Small businesses that provide the majority of jobs and wealth to some people are developed by entrepreneurially minded individuals, many of these people ceaselessly exploring various ways to improve the business. Most of the people that have exposure to entrepreneurship are often having the courage to do something without boundaries for themselves, having higher self-esteem, and an overall better sense of control for their own lives.

Although most of us have the natural ability to learn a certain subject or discipline, we can also improve our skills if we have the willingness to learn new things and enough time to mold ourselves into a precious stone. Therefore it is important that there is an entrepreneurial partner with more knowledge that could help you to develop a business. And it also helps you to learn about key business areas like sales, marketing, finance, management and accountancy, And as well as extensive practice such as effective communication, adaptability, good interactions with other people and building self-esteem.

This book allows us to use practical insights into the wealth of knowledge to guide us how to become an entrepreneur. As I am forming as a young entrepreneur and experiencing different situations in the line of business, I've learned that some books offer some great advice that will greatly help to give a brief advice to my mentees. By telling my personal stories and relating those of other successful entrepreneurs. I made a book that the main core of the topic focuses on the key lessons that can be a guide to young entrepreneurs who cannot simply be seen in some textbooks, online books or magazines.

Furthermore, one of the main reasons why I made this book was to help young entrepreneurs to avoid some mistakes in a business that I also had been experience when I was just getting started. Mistakes during the early days just like a bad decision such as spending too much money or having a bad business partner can be devastating and could lead to an entrepreneur having to shut down operations completely. After I made some of bad decision and mistakes, I would often think about, "I wish there were a book where I can get advice or hint what might be the outcome of my decision". And now this book already exists, and I can help people who have the same wish and experiencing the same problem as I was before. This book is divided into seven parts: Business Strategy, Think Big, Mindset of successful entrepreneur, the harsh reality of entrepreneurial world and How to avoid the lonely life of an entrepreneur. Each topic contains a variety of ideas and subjects that can greatly help each entrepreneur that can read separately or sequentially. You can focus your interest on what topic is most helpful to you and based on your own interests or you can also read the book from beginning to end. You will find the great value in reading this book whether you are planning to build your own business, approaching five years in business, or celebrating the first year of business. In other words, it can help you to develop the Entrepreneur Mind.

What does it Mean to be Entrepreneurial?

Did you know that the word "entrepreneur" came from the French word entrepedre, which means "Undertaker" as the definition of a person working on a major project. Jean Baptise Say is one of the French economists that is most popular for coining this term around 1800, which emphasized "the entrepreneur moves resources from areas with lower and in an area with high productivity and greater yield" (Drucker 1985a: 23).In other words, the creation of value is the embodiment of entrepreneurship. Yet, the meaning continues to change over the years. Schumpeter is probably one of the best known for devising the word "Creative destruction" in 1942, where it emphasizes "new" entrepreneurship elements in new innovations to replace existing products, services and processes. According to Schumpeter, the main role of an entrepreneur is to change or make changes to the design of a product. By utilizing an invention, or more generally,

An untested technological possibility for creating a new equipment or creating an old one in innovative ways, By developing a new source of supply of a product or a new channel for products, by establishing an industry and so on. Thereby, suggesting that entrepreneurship can take many different forms or combinations. For example, henry ford, the founder of the Ford Motor Company who installed the first assembly line technique of mass production for automobiles, created more efficient and cost-effective process.

Business Strategy

Usually businesses with a good and solid strategy are the ones that remain successful and ready to win. For too many entrepreneurs, often strategies are only given attention when business errors occur. That's why before we build a business we must ask ourselves three vital questions related to our business strategy: Where are we now? Where do we want to be? How do we get there? If you do not know the answer to these questions you probably do not have the strategy to be successful. In other words, you have an action that has no purpose to succeed, not well planned, no chances of survival and a likely failure on your hands.

There are cases where large companies are being beaten by small companies not just because of good product quality, it is also due to strategy that being analyze before it was implemented, "while the grasshopper rest on their laurels, the ants are implementing and executing a better strategy". The strategy and tactics of a company will greatly help to overcome every obstacle that may cause its downfall. In this chapter you will have an idea of what strategies and tactics you can use to improve your business and it covers from devising an exit plan by testing a new market. It will set up your business ahead of the rest if you spend enough time studying and mastering its important concepts.

I. The Three Major Reasons for New Business Failure

Most businesses built by entrepreneurs have the same objective to be successful someday, however the unfortunate truth are, some of them are no longer reaching that point which often leads to business shutdown. There are various reasons why new businesses may fail. Identifying the major causes helps you avoid the misstep common to many new entrepreneurs. Some of the reasons why a business fails before it reaches the pull potential are because of lack of planning, insufficient funding and overreaching. In this chapter we will give you some meaningful advice on how to avoid this failure before it happens to you.

A. *Lack of planning*

Often the reason why an entrepreneur builds a business is because of their passion for it and is likely to be centered on a product or service that they know and love, and many excellent advices are not being addressed, believing that their passion and creativity is the most important component in order to grow. But business plans are not just like a small store where you just need to insert a little effort and perseverance in order to become successful. The business plan will be the basis of every entrepreneur to understand the market, which they will be ahead of all competitors and how many valued customers they need to succeed. Business plan will also explain step by step the relationship between operating expenses including overall prices and profits where all the information needed by an entrepreneur to setting out a business's future goals and strategies. Some of the small businesses often fail because the owners do not spend time and research on a business plan to avoid mistakes which may cause business shutdown.

B. *Insufficient funding (Undercapitalization)*

When you're planning to build a business or start as a new owner of a business, research and planning is really necessary. Undercapitalization can be the main problem of an entrepreneur while in the middle of a career, which one of the reasons why a business would lead to bankruptcy. In fact you do not necessarily need to spend a lot of money to start a business; all you need is the strategy and tactics on how to improve it beyond the very few resources. Just like an apple computer started in a garage of steve wozniak and steve jobs. UPS (United parcel service) was started because of the 100 dollars borrowed by jim casey to his friend in 1907. To help fellow students a pair of Stanford University graduate students, Jerry Yang and David flow was founded "YAHOO" to locate cool web sites that would greatly help each student in their study. There is nothing wrong with this approach if you want to keep the business work successfully as long as you're ready to spend a great amount of time and energy for it. But always keep in mind that under capitalization is the number one problems of starting up businesses, so do not skimp getting enough money to start your business based on the plans you made.

C. Over reaching

Another reason for the failure of small businesses is the over expansion. Without a plan or strategy for expansion, you may have trouble with the accurate inventory to satisfy the immediate demands. The new business is usually popular at first because it gets a lot of attention to their customer, and owners may suddenly discover a lot of ideas and opportunities that he or she can use to improve their products and services. However, some owners are taking a chance on every opportunity to expand sales without consideration for the right kind of management and basic quality controls in place and this will lead to investments of all their working capital to expand their business without any studies done for new ideas and markets. In addition, the reliance on a few customers for the majority of your income is too risky because it also means that you are entering the kind of situation where you can fall as soon as they decide to leave your business. These types of methods put some small businesses into possible risk that could lead to shut down. Even if you're busy handling some valued customers or customers pays for your products that provide most of your income, you should have some plans to further expand your client base to support your company's primary source of business especially to those potential customers which have a high likelihood of becoming customers. Some of the successful businesses are gradually growing along with good product quality, management controls and good services. An idea where you can start thinking about how to grow your business is when it already has a solid foundation towards progress and you're making a profit from the products and services you sell to customers

Almost all businesses define the development through increased sales, but it's also important to focus on how to maintain or improve your profitability

II. Things you must do to improve your business:

A. Make some ways to increase your sales, both to existing customers and new customers

B. Doing some research and testing for improving your product and services to your customers

C. Developing new products and services that can be popular in the new or existing market

D. Perform some training on your current staff, including working with trainees and mentors.

E. Find additional sources of funding just like bringing some investors

F. Make some way to sell your product and services like selling it thru online

G. Consult with some professional business mentors who will be very helpful to you as to how things can be done without any mistakes

III. "Think Big"

In business, thinking big means showing the ability to generate an idea to maximize the scope of your full potential. Similarly, it can also mean generating ideas that have a great impact on the business world. In spite of its simple definition, thinking big is not as easy to do for many reasons, but if you know already the obstacles that you could encounter you can avoid them altogether.

A. *The inability to outgrow environment*

I am a mentor to many young entrepreneurs, and the inability to create businesses beyond the limits of their reality or environment is one of the common failures I often experience in them. In other words, their environment is limiting their minds to come up with an idea that is reaching the point that their business is suffering from limited growth or even death.

To counter the effects on young entrepreneurs, here are some examples of entrepreneur that step outside the boundary of their environment to become successful. For example there are many college student that wish to build their business which focusing only those college students on their campus. Instead, I give them some ideas on how to improve their business, such as applying their product or service to another business group. For example, try to leave your comfort zone and do not just limit the products and services to your campus, there are many colleges across the nation or the world that you could sell your product. If this idea has had a big impact on people, it may be even bigger than you expected. Also, I share with my college mentees that the Facebook's cofounder Mark Zuckerberg starts with an idea that social media is made for college students only, was originated on an ideology that appeals to people all around the world. It takes a long time before face book Facebook's co-founder Mark Zuckerberg made an idea to expand his company's target from college students to all the people of the world.

B. Lack of motivation to pursue big ideas

The lack of willingness to pursue bigger ideas is one of the mentalities that I often see among entrepreneurs who have had some level of monetary success in business. These entrepreneurs keep the business in their comfort zone or in an idea without even trying to level up. As business author Michael Gerber says, "The comfort makes us cowardly to try something else". Furthermore, these types of entrepreneurs are likely to be overwhelmed with running of their own business and may not be able to deal with this situation to do anything else. I know that staying motivated is difficult for entrepreneur, In order to overcome the lack of motivation, entrepreneurs should seek for an individual or group to push and support him to continue their ideas, step by step. Also, having someone holding me accountable for my goals is very helpful. Moreover, like other entrepreneurs having several businesses, In order to develop your idea you need to carve out priority time and assigned tasks to others.

C. *Lack the self-confidence*

They do not see themselves handling a big organization which operates based on their ideas that they have implemented or see themselves managing large group of people. Some of the questions that most of entrepreneur may ask themselves are: How do I start? Where I can find a team that is capable of pulling things off? Where I can get big capital to execute my idea for my business? In order to boost your self-confidence, create and make small steps that start you working on your idea. For example, start to make some study about your idea or write down some important information to support your idea. If you are going to be aggressive in finding some information that will help you to do your ideas well, these small steps will add up to increase your confidence and to push you forward

D. Lack the diversity and expertise

Did you ever watch the television show "Shark tank" in which entrepreneurs set up their business idea into a group of investors, or sharks, where they choose an entrepreneur to put their investment with Presenting Company. Entrepreneurs who appear on the show look for investment capital as much as the valuable experience of the sharks. In one episode, the shark has a suggestion to the entrepreneur to license his product rather than to sell it to individual retailers, which is difficult process. The entrepreneur did not think that one of the strategies that would give him faster income and minimize the risk would be the licensing of his product. In this case like many others, the experience and influence of seasoned entrepreneurs in order to maximize the potential of a business idea is essential for the founders

To jump this hurdle, you need to establish various networks of individuals who can think big and having the ability to understand every aspect of entrepreneurship to get to that level. Likewise, this will be great help for you to evaluate and improve your idea. The founder of "LinkedIn" Reid Hoffman, recently stated to a group of aspiring entrepreneurs in Cambridge, England, — Talk and get ideas for as many people as possible. From here you will have an idea what is wrong with your idea and what else you need to change or do to improve it. They can guide you to learn more.

IV.   Mindset of successful entrepreneur

They say one of the reasons for the success of most entrepreneurs is their mindset, the ability to deal and overcome every problem that will throw to them.

Sometimes when we look in every successful entrepreneur we only see their fame and the achievements they have. But before they experience this kind of acknowledgement they first went through difficulties, suffering, tear, roadblocks and the trials they have overcome to get where they are now. But what sets some of the world's most successful entrepreneur apart from others is their ability to deal with any problem and continue to fight even when everything seems to be going against them. The fears and challenges listed below are common feelings or being experienced by most of us, But we have to overcome them in able for us to reach our full potential of success.

A. *Criticism*

We as people often want to be great in every sense of the word and our chosen line of expertise. We always thirst for compliments and desires for a moment where we can truly be proud of. It may be in the line of business, sports, acting, academics and even creating some things that you can put your heart into and run with. But in long life journey, circumstances may change and Many of us are allowed to be affected by criticisms of naysayers which reduce the enthusiasm to those dreams that we set forth to achieve. One of the biggest mistakes an entrepreneur can do is worrying too much about what other people think of them, about their ideas or their business. Instead of allowing criticism to waste our time by thinking too much and roll off our shoulders, we must use it as a way to improve ourselves and do not let it stop us from moving forward and doing the things we believe in. The criticism and haters are often used by successful entrepreneurs to fuel them to make things much better instead of taking it to heart. Although some of the feedback and criticism could help us to know what we need to improve and make things right, it also has a way of knocking us down and second guessing ourselves. Grow thick skin, and push through even when others stop you to do so. Imagine how great it will feel when you prove to them that they are wrong. Don't be afraid to step outside of your comfort zone. Greatness is not located within the areas of your comfort zone. You have to continue to push harder for your desired success. Just keep going despite the naysayers. Some people are going to talk until you lose hope and passion to continue. They can call you a stupid, tell you you're just wasting your time, tell you that you are not fit for this job; you can only be a burden to others! They'll doubt you. However it is still up to you if you react to what they say or use it as fuel to further improve everything. The greatest names in history are those who do not want to allow the criticism of other people to determine their destiny.

Whatever happens or can happen to your chosen line of expertise or something you love most. Just keep on it. Fight for it, accept any punches that may be given to you but do not faint or just give up and come back for round two. Soon enough, people who judge you will be recognizing your praises after realizing that you're truly dedicated to what it is that you love

B. *Failure*

As a normal person we are all afraid of failure, whether you're an entrepreneur or not, because no one wants to fail. Our natural instincts are to be successful in everything, and Because of our willingness to avoid failing and making mistakes, we always find ourselves asking the age old question of: "What if?" If we concentrate our energy on thinking about all the things that could go wrong, we often lose sight of all the things that could go right. Most of the successful entrepreneur doesn't concentrate on failure. Instead, they concentrate on success. Although it is natural for a person to make a mistake and have some obstacles along the way, rather than staying here, you must learn from it, and continue to move on.

If you are a businessman, you can't avoid that at one point you will fail. This is the nature of a business which has never been successful in the beginning. Whether that failure is big or small, it has a lesson you can learn from. Failures are often viewed as the end, but that doesn't have to be the real case. For most entrepreneurs and their businesses, failure is just another chapter of their life and it serves as a lesson where you can further improve it. If you found yourself failing at first, it's time to pivot and find a better solution to the problem. Just know that failure is an option or maybe you need to start over from scratch. The failure occurs on your journey is a stepping stone on the path to success. You need to gather new information along the way that will help you to avoid mistakes.

Some of you may have heard about "overnight success", but in most cases, these stories are mostly about the great things that have been done in the course of success and often they don't reveal the missteps behind the eventual achievements. For instance, researchers and engineers often invent thousands of failed machines or technologies before they finally make one that works. Likewise, entrepreneurs often start various businesses and products before they can find a formula that result in profits. Some business owners, on the other hand, are so afraid of making failure to the point that they're weaken with fear. The fear they feel is preventing them from acting, pivoting, creating, and founding. If you find yourself afraid of failure, try to look for acceptance.

C. *Offending Others*

Recently I was reading an article on how our generation today can prevent of being offended by everything. We live in a generation where every person often finds something to be offended about, and through social media with accessibility to reach the wide audience around the world people have the courage to be more vocal than ever But the worst thing that you could ever do is to sit back and do not do anything, or let yourself stop doing something you believe because you might offend someone else.

As an entrepreneur you have to stop being afraid of every other person's thinking about you, if you want to see success do not let yourself take control of other people's opinions about you. If you are just working to try to stand out and impress everyone, you're fighting an impossible battle

D. *The Past and the Future*

You cannot go back and change the past and you can't control the future. When you begin to realize this thing, you are setting yourself up for success.

Living in the present moment does not just allow you to do the best in life, but also preparing yourself for success. You will not focus on being successful today if your mind still going back to the past or thinking of what might happen in the future, life is now don't waste your time to think negative things which may knock you down.

Successful people make peace in their past and look at it as a lesson of your life today which will help to build your future. They also embrace the uncertainty of their future, because the constant thinking in the future will only prevent them to live happily and prevent them from living in the moment.

E. *Negativity*

You have two choices in life, sit down and waste the time to complain why something did not happen based on what you planned, or you stand upright, learn your mistakes, and keep moving forward. Constant complaining about how things does not happen based on what you plan or should have happened according to your plan will not get you anywhere. I would always say that you cannot complain to an event or thing where you have the ability to change.

Successful entrepreneur don't sit on one side and feel sorry for themselves because something did not happen based on what they wanted or did not go their way, instead they look at what things and circumstances they should be thankful for and radiate positivity, even when it may feel like they are faking it until they make it. They don't have time for negative people in their lives, or even negative in themselves.

So I challenge you, can you overcome the above challenges or just let yourself be defeated in all the challenges of life?

V.   The harsh reality of entrepreneurial world

There's always comment about the end game in the form of an accomplishment, announcements about funding, or final flame out. Hollywood has even created a movie about how Facebook started and its founding where great attention was given to the glamorization of startup life instead of showing what it really is. We rarely hear about the harsh facts that entrepreneur often encounters on their journey before they reach the success they are experiencing right now. This is not meant to be included in this article to be a downbeat, but in reality it is just the opposite. By knowing the harsh reality that awaits to you. You can be prepared for every obstacle you can encounter in the middle of your career. Here are some of the harsh realities you can experience in the field of being an entrepreneur

A. *Expect that the first iteration of an idea is wrong*

There are many cases that the first implementation or iteration of your ideas is often wrong. It does not mean that your decisions are wrong, you are not doing the right thing, or for whatever reason which cause to fall hard to yourself. As it turns out, in fact this is a good sign for you, because there is no idea that will be accepted immediately on your first customer interaction and it requires some feedback and suggestions from them to match their needs. You could be stubborn, do not listen to any suggestions provided by your customer, and keep things the way they were. In the end, your customers will be forced to quit because the products you are supplying do not suit their need. It's okay if things change up a little when it comes to your idea and its implementation

B. *Your family or friends can't understand you no matter what you do*

"You're an entrepreneur, so that means you do not have your own job?" or "Oh that's nice" some of the many reaction you get from your closest friends, family members, and other people while you're in the middle of starting your company. The sad truth is people still won't understand what you do even if you some achievements that are worthy of praise and shows a significant success in the entrepreneurial world. Unless you have made some things that will have an impact on your consumer success stories that come around every few years, maybe things will not change from here. Just like b2b space where most of the people are not your customers so it's harder to explain your service to them, especially if it's a niche workflow. It simply means there is more outside in the world than just techies and entrepreneurs where these is okay and sometimes even a relief to know. It does not mean that they do not understand it mean that you are doing something wrong and not acceptable to others.

C. *You will make a small wage for a while*

If you enter the entrepreneurial world because of the big return of your money, then you are in the wrong business. Surely you will sell your company when it first grows up, but that day is far far away and do not expect that you can do it in just 1 to 2 years. Although usually there are earn out clauses, vesting still complete, and a whole lot more. Even if you are having a good chunk of cash, your money will be better spent on the best talents than paying a high wage yourself. There's nothing wrong with the desire to earn money if you've been working on it. But in the beginning it will not be easy. If you really like what you are doing and have a passion for it, the capacity to have a large bank account requires gallons of fuel for your engine to complete your mission. Everyone is sure that basic creature comforts are needed, but expensive things look silly because you will not have the time to really enjoy them.

D. *You Can't Do It All Yourself*

Some entrepreneurs become arrogant sometimes where they think they can do everything without help from others or with just one co-founder. They think that two or three people are enough to scale the company. This results only by overworked and taking a lot of time for your work. You should know how to let your pride go out and find someone who is often better than you. To encourage others to work for you, there is also the ability for each team member to give particular attention to what they are best at.

E. *There's no such thing as an overnight success*

For many reasons you will know that your idea will not work unexpectedly or that you are one of the lucky few that get acquired early on. Another thing is that you are ready to work for a long time. The press often indicates that success can be obtained in just overnight, but in reality the entrepreneur themselves spent a long time in a company for so many years. You need to spend a lot of time and effort to establish your business. Some of the successful businesses spend around 5 to 10 years to ensure that its operations and operations are stable. At first it was difficult but it was worth to wait. Startups aren't a 5k, but an all-out iron man competition.

F. *There are things that are not covered by your control*

Last but not the least; you have to understand that you cannot control anything in this world. The market you see today may shut down the next day; the beautiful forest can be destroyed by the storm, and other unforeseen circumstances. Do not let this happening affects you and let this make you quit. It's like barricades in a concert, sports game, or party that you want to get to. You can wait for traffic or find an alternative route to get to your destination, you will be able to get to your destination as long as you are determined to get. In the words of the late randy pausch "the brick wall is there to show you how hard you will be if you want something". Once again, these tips do not mean that we are preventing you from becoming an entrepreneur, but we just want to know if you're mentally, emotionally and spiritually ready for all business trials and check to make sure you're prepared. Some of the companies die because people just give up . I hope that this book has given you some ideas on how to prevent the problems that you may encounter in the middle of your career. Being an entrepreneur is really hard, but if you really love what you are doing and your determination for it, you WILL do it.

VI.   How to avoid the lonely life of an entrepreneur

Along the entrepreneurial journey no one knows that it was easy as what others think. Although we're bombarded with success stories left, right and center,

Inspirational message and motivation workshops, you seldom receive the story about the people who fail, or give up, or feel so lonesome they quit and go back to their office job so they can have light water cooler conversation day by day (do individuals even do that?). It's lonely at first. As your business and ideas grow, your life will begin to change quickly, and it feels like a fast moving car you're struggling to hold into. There's no hesitation that being an entrepreneur, it can be a pretty lonely road. In fact, as a creative kind of person, Loneliness is the feeling you cannot avoid on your journey, sometimes we need to be alone to think, to absorb and to construct ideas. I do not say that creative entrepreneurs are all hermits with social anxiety.

Being entrepreneur having to work late nights, spend time at work even on weekends, taking risk alone, continue to believe in his vision even no one else believes in you, and even skipping to attend some important occasions and holidays for the sake of his business are the path that they choose where they are always alone.

Based on the new study conducted by researchers from at the University of North Carolina shows that loneliness is constantly puts a person's risk of heart disease, cancer and stroke, it also weakens your health where you become susceptible to diseases such as diabetes, high blood pressure and more.

The research evaluated loneliness through several life stages, but the overall result is clear: loneliness can kill. This advice is cheap, and easy to ignore, just like the entrepreneur, but I'll try anyway. There are ways to avoid loneliness, or at least remove some of its killing power. Here are just a few:

A. *Choose a good community*

It is important to have a group of interconnected people just like you. By building a community with other founders will help you to inspire and remedies loneliness. This can also be a physical or a virtual community. Naija startup offers some great virtual platforms for entrepreneurs, not just for the network but also for learning and gain inspiration or even having impact on other business owners.

B. *Collaborate*

Normal for every person to feel lonely from time to time, but for some, the loneliness they feel is more often. Feeling lonely can be difficult for other people, such as the elderly, those who are far from their loved ones, and those who experience depression. If your personal instinct is to live alone, you run the risk of self-imposed isolation, which may cause your depression, Although depression does not always lead to loneliness, but the feeling of being alone can be the root of depression one year or even two years later, and it certainly leads to sadness over time, "As Dr. Hawkley says. Freeing yourself of feeling like being isolated by depression is a big step or healing process to cure you to depression. So Instead of separating yourself from others, find a partner or co-founder who will greatly help you. For one thing, you will have someone you can talk to and guide you towards your success. Second, it gives you the opportunity to find someone capable of adapting to the quality you are looking for as a partner. For example you are a tech whiz, so you need someone who knows the marketing and skilled about it.

True, sometimes having a partner sometimes sucks, and it is unavoidable to realize that even if the founder needs to be fired down the line, but it can also be a perfect, productive relationship.

C. *Relationship is always your priority*

Forbes.com says: "You must prioritize your relationship, although at the very beginning it might be uncomfortable to you. As an entrepreneur, it's hard for you to balance the entrepreneurial hustle while you trying to build friendship to everyone. Keep up the relationship that shows you the value in maintaining long term. Although there is nothing wrong with acquaintances or new friends, but you will be more rationally satisfied by maintaining a core group of friends and investing the time to maintain a good relationship with them – not developing too many relationships that you inherently forfeit depth." They couldn't have said it well.

D. *Co-working spaces*

Sometimes co-working spaces can be distracted for business owners. However, there are some co-working spaces that you can work alone (whether it is a private office or a booth) but still, in the middle of that place there are varieties of other businesses within the same space or building. This will also mean that you can retreat to work or network / socialize whenever you want.

E. Be more assertive and having forceful personality

Not only does this help you prioritize more when it comes to your relationship but the opportunity cost of saying 'yes' to everything which means that this person is more important in your life . Your partner or spouse, close friends, family and relatives, take the back seat. As a busy businessman we have plenty of time to do our job. Whether it is certain associations or the calendar obligations you are about to make, it is better to say NO to the good so you have time for the great.

F. Learn from your mentor

Your mentor is likely to have experience your problems which have been down a similar road and has successfully overcome it. Therefore it is better to talk with him not only about things about business or cerebral stuff but also about life and strategies for balancing a healthy life and dealing with loneliness.

G. *Be true to yourself*

It's easy to pretend and show a behavior that is contrary to your true nature and to get lost when trying to mesh within a community. Non-authenticity as an entrepreneur is the worst thing you could ever do in your business. In an effort to avoid loneliness, it is important to remember that the gift you received is different from those of others. Often the insatiable desire to create or innovate is can be both a curse and blessing of a businessman. So, stay authentic

ABOUT THE AUTHOR

Markus Edison Goldberg is one of the co-founder of "Future Innovation" whose programs and services in insight, entrepreneurial mindset and thinking-based change permanently improve a large organization's ability to innovate. He teaches Professional Entrepreneurship at the St. Daniel School of Management, MIT, and has co-authored a number of books and articles on entrepreneurship and insight including "small business management".

Markus first book, Global entrepreneur, was a number one New York best seller. A fellow at the American institute, he is also the founding editor of national business online and has been nominated for two consecutive years as Americas fifty most influential entrepreneur for a Pulitzer price. The main advocacy of Markus is to give ideas and guidance to young aspiring entrepreneurs who can help them to overcome every challenge of the entrepreneurial world.

www.ingramcontent.com/pod-product-compliance
Lightning Source LLC
Chambersburg PA
CBHW070519220526
45467CB00002B/740